META TAGS

Optimising Your Website for Internet Search Engines

(Google, Yahoo!, MSN, AltaVista, AOL, Alltheweb, Fast, GigaBlast, Netscape, Snap, WISEnut and Others)

Samuel Blankson

ISBN 10: 1-905789-98-X
ISBN 13: 978-1-905789-98-6

First Published by Lulu Inc in 2007

Contents

Introduction

Buying a website is only the start of finding success on the internet. Next you have to be found by web users. Being found on Google, Yahoo!, MSN, AltaVista, AOL, Alltheweb, Fast, GigaBlast, Netscape, Snap, WISEnut and thousands of other search engines is the next major hurdle you have to climb. Whilst offline advertising can help, it can be very expensive – and depending on your website – this may be too localized for a global market.

You could use online advertising. Again, this is useful and effective if carefully planned; however, it can be time consuming and also expensive. There are other avenues such as blogs, press releases, affiliation, banner exchange and link exchange to name but a few. All these methods have their place in your overall marketing plan; however, before you even start all that, you need to optimize your website so that web users searching through search engines like Google, Yahoo!, MSN, AltaVista, AOL, Alltheweb, Fast, GigaBlast, Netscape, Snap, WISEnut and thousands of smaller search engines, can quickly find you. This means optimizing your website so that it will be found on the first search results page and preferably in the top ten highest ranking results.

The search engine is the most popular way that web users find information online. The term for getting a site more visible on the internet through search engines is called Search Engine Optimization (SEO). SEO is the means by which you make your website more visible to the outside world. The start of any serious SEO project is internal website optimization. By first optimizing your websites title, headings, Meta Tags, other tags (links, images, files etc), and the actual webpage contents' text, you will be able to maximize the effectiveness of how search engines view and rank your websites' relevance to keyword searches.

This is where this book on Meta Tags comes into play. In the pages of this book you will learn all you need to know about Meta Tags.

We will examine what Meta Tags are, what each tag does, and how you can use them effectively to enhance your website ranking with search engines.

What Are Meta Tags

Your web pages have an underlying code that represents the entire webpage through a coded language. This coded language is called Hyper Text Markup Language (HTML or XHTML, an extended version which requires tags to be properly closed). HTML uses tags to represent everything you see on a webpage (see Appendix 2 in the appendices on page 77). There are some main tags we will now examine in order to better understand Meta Tags.

The first tag in most web pages is the HTML tag. This tag is represented with *<HTML>* and has to be closed at the end of your web page with *</HTML>*. The / represents an end to the tag name that follows it. In HTML, declared tags need to be closed with the / followed by the tag name.

You have to have *<HTML>* at the beginning of your website code. If you don't have *<HTML>* at the beginning of your webpage code, everything else you declare within the webpage code may appear as text in the browser.

The next tag is the Head tag. This is where we will concentrate the bulk of this book. The *<HEAD>* section specifies information about the website and webpage for search engines. Apart from the Title tag described next, information specified in the Head section will not be visibly displayed on your webpage when viewed through a web browser. We will look closely at all the tags that come under the head section. These tags declare information that helps search engines to index, rank, categorize, and cross-reference web pages. They also define character sets, author name, copyright information, page title, and keywords as well as whether the page should be revisited or cached by search engines.

The Title Tag tells the browser the page title. This is displayed on the title line of the browser. This should ideally be less than sixty Characters. Titles longer than this may not be fully displayed by some web browsers.

Special script code like JavaScript and other types of scripts can be specified with the *<SCRIPTS>* tag (see Appendix 2, in the appendices on page 77 for a full listing of all the available tags).

The next HTML section is the bulk of most web pages. It is the *<BODY>* section. This section contains all the text, tables, images, sound, forms etc.

So now you know the various sections of a HTML coded webpage, let us look at the original question we asked at the beginning of this section, "What are Meta Tags?" Meta Tags are optional tags containing information inserted under the *<HEAD>* section of your web pages. These are called Meta Tags because they define a tag rather than being tags themselves. Apart from the Title tag, all tags specified under the *<HEAD>* section are Meta Tags. Meta Tags tell search engines how to handle, index rank and display your web pages. This information goes towards helping search engines rank your pages, and website.

If you submit your web site to search engines, your website would eventually be visited by the search engine spider programs or robots. These would proceed to index your pages. The way each of the search engines spider programs works differs slightly from search engine to search engine. For instance, some search engines like AltaVista will index everything from your web pages. However it will only generate a description from the first 250 characters. Therefore if your web pages do not start with a page description, AltaVista will instead continue to describe it with whatever you have at the beginning of your site. This could be useless descriptions that say nothing about the content that a visitor may find on the site. It therefore is wise to include a page description as the first paragraph of each webpage. Therefore make sure that your opening paragraph is carefully written and it accurately reflects what the page contains.

What does a Meta Tag look like?

Not all search engines support Meta Tags. Excite for instance doesn't. However it is still prudent to use Meta Tags as many of the other major search engines do support them and your Meta Tags allow you to exert some level of control over how these search engines index and treat your site.

You can insert the Meta Tag element after the Title Tag; however you should always start with the <HTML> Meta Tag. The <TITLE> element can be declared within your <HTML> Meta Tag.

There are two types of Meta Tag attributes. A Meta Tag declaration resembles either of the following:

    <META HTTP-EQUIV="name" CONTENT="content">
    <META NAME="name" CONTENT="content">

Meta Tags with an HTTP-EQUIV attribute control the action of browsers, and may be used to refine the information provided by the actual headers, thus they are equivalent to HTTP Headers. Meta Tags using this form should have an equivalent effect when specified as an HTTP Header, and on some servers may automatically be translated into actual HTTP Headers or by a pre-processing tool on the server.

HTTP-EQUIV META tags work with most browsers but may not work with all. They may not be understood by cache agents and proxies, therefore wherever possible, use the HTTP Headers instead. Wherever an HTTP-EQUIV META Tag is listed in this book, its associated HTTP Header will also be given.

In HTML, Meta Tag definitions do not need to be closed with </, however you should not include any line breaks in your declaration of the Meta Tag. This can cause your webpage to be incorrectly read by the search engine spider programs.

The following are a few examples of Meta Tag declarations:

Examples
How to define web page keywords:
<meta name="keywords"content="Meta Tag,MetaTag,Meta Tags,MetaTags,Book,Books,MetaTag Book,MetaTag Books">

How to define a web page description:
<meta name="description"content="A book on MetaTags and using Meta Tags.">

How to set the last revision of your page:
<meta name="revised"content="MetaTags,20/09/2007">

How to Refresh a page every 5 seconds:
<meta http-equiv="refresh" content="5">

Required Attributes

The following are required attributes for declaring Meta Tags.

DTD indicates in which document type the attribute is allowed. S=Strict, T=Transitional, and F=Frameset.

Attribute	Value	Description	DTD
	content	Some text	Defines meta information to be associated with http-equiv or name	STF

Optional Attributes

The following are optional attributes for declaring Meta Tags.

Attribute	Value	Description	DTD
http-equiv	content-type expires refresh set-cookie	Connects the content attribute to an HTTP Header	STF
name	author description keywords generator revised others	Connects the content attribute to a name	STF
scheme	Some text	Defines a format to be used to interpret the value of the content attribute	STF

Standard Attributes

The following are standard attributes for declaring Meta Tags.

dir, lang, xml:lang

The Title Tag

As you previously read, the HTML title tag is not a Meta Tag. It is a HTML tag and as such it could be defined outside the Head section and still function, however it is worth grouping it under the Head section. You should specify your website title within the *<TITLE>* and *</TITLE>* tags.

How Do Search Engines Use This Tag

Almost all search engines use the Title Tag for ranking purpose and most of them use it as a listing title for your webpage. Therefore it is critical that you make this title tag work hard for you.

Here is where your first bit of SEO comes in. Search engines such as Google use the information in the Title tag to determine the relevance of your site to keyword searches; therefore, it is a good idea to make sure this information is as SEO friendly as possible and if possible, make it contain your webpage and website's main keywords.

Spend some time to select the best and most popular keywords for your website and webpage content. Use a keyword suggestion tool to tunnel down into these keywords to find the most popular and relevant sub-keywords. Then make up your title.

To create an SEO friendly title, use a keyword tool such as, http://www.iwebtool.com/keyword_suggestion.

Keyword suggestion tools are ideal for finding the most popular keywords for your website. Simply input the main keyword and press the return key on your keyboard. You will be presented with suggestions of related keywords. Select the most relevant keyword in the highest ranking position and click on the link for that keyword. This will take you to a dead end or it will suggest further keywords. Continue this till you have four to six keywords. Then make up your title with these. You can separate them with '|' or '–'or ','. Remember to keep the title to less than sixty characters.

Any text you place within the <TITLE> and </TITLE> tags will be displayed on the title bar of the web browser the page is viewed on. Some web browsers append extra text to the title such as Microsoft Internet Explorer.

The following example shows how you can create a title from keywords.

Title Tag Example

meta tags
meta tags html
meta tags generator
meta tags Google
meta tags keywords
meta tags in html
meta tags robots
meta tags tutorial
meta tags description
meta tags seo
meta tags analyzer

The above keywords could be used to create the following Title Tag for a Meta Tag SEO website.

<TITLE> Meta Tags in HTML | Keywords and Description Generator | SEO Tutorial | Google Robots Analyzer | </TITLE>

Meta Description Tag

AltaVista and **InfoSeek** support this Meta Tag.

The Meta Description Tag defines a general description of what is contained within your webpage. Some search engines use this information, along with the Title Tag, to create a brief description of your webpage in their search results. The Meta Description Tag is particularly important if your document is a frameset, has extensive scripts at the top, or has very little text.

The Meta Description Tag allows you to influence the description of your page in the search engines that support the tag. Search engines that support Meta Tags will often display the Description Meta Tag along with your title in their results.

Google ignores the Meta Description Tag and instead will automatically generate its own description for web pages. Other search engines may support it partially. For instance, Teoma displays the first portion of the page's description using the Meta Description tag, then displays the pages rank in the search and then displays the remaining portion by drawing from the body of the page itself.

How to use this Meta Tag

META Name: "Description"
General Usage: *<META   name="Description"   content="Your description">*

Your description text should go between the quotation marks after the content= portion of the Meta Description Tag. This should not be longer than 200 to 250 characters, as most of the search engines that use this Meta Tag will only index descriptions up to this length. Generally however, only twenty words from your description will be displayed with search results, therefore make sure that the first ten to twenty words of your description contains the "hook", to capture the search engine user's attention. You can use the remainder of your description to further expand on your webpage's purpose and content.

Whilst it may be worthwhile to use the Meta Description Tag for your webpage's for the degree of control it gives you with various search engines, it can be time consuming to create effective descriptions for each page, therefore you may want to limit using the Meta Description Tag to only the critical, most popular and important pages on your website. You may also wish to reuse Meta Descriptions for pages with similar or identical content. This is especially useful if your site changes regularly, you add pages continuously to your site or if your site has a lot of pages.

Meta Description Tag Example

If your site sold accounting software and you offered a trial version through the site, you could use the free offer as a hook in your Meta Description Tag.

Instead of starting your description with the following:
<META name="Description" content="A site that specializes in accounting software.">

You could instead start your description with the following:
<META name="Description" content="Download free accounting software here. ">

You will note that "Download" and "Free" are very popular search keywords on the internet.

Meta Abstract Tag

The Meta Abstract Tag can be used to define a brief abstraction of your website. This Meta Tag is often confused with the Meta Description Tag; however, they are very different.

The Meta Abstract Tag is an abstraction or a brief summary of the Meta Description Tag. This Meta Tag is best kept short and brief. A single line description of the entire webpage is best. The Meta Abstract Tag is hardly used by search engines; however, for the search engines that read the first few lines of text of your web pages, it is useful.

How to use this Meta Tag

META Name: "Abstract"

General Usage: *<META name="Abstract" content="Abstract phrase">*

How Search Engines Use This Meta Tag

This Meta Tag is almost useless for the purposes of raising your search engine ranking. The first reason for this is that hardly any search engines use it and secondly, the ones that do, generally use it for enhancing their archiving and indexing rather than for ranking purposes.

Although not many search engines look specifically for the Abstract Meta Tag, it adds a generalization of your webpage into your page's headers which search engines read often when archiving web pages.

The following is an example of how you can create a Meta Abstract Tag:

Meta Abstract Tag Example

*<META name="Abstract" content="Meta Abstract Tag
description and example.">*

Meta Author Tag

The Meta Author Tag declares who the author of the document is. This Meta Tag is unsupported by most search engines. It defines the name, email address of the author, company name or web address (URL).

How to use this Meta Tag

META Name: "Author"
General *<META name="Author" content="Author*
Usage: *Information">*

How Search Engines Use This Meta Tag

Again this Meta Tag will in no way aid your page's rise to the top of the search engine rankings, as not many search engines look specifically for the Meta Author Tag. However the Meta Author Tag clearly defines who the author is and/or the responsible party for making updates to the webpage. Therefore it is good practice to include it.

Most web authoring software will allow you to specify this Meta Tag. The software then automatically inserts the tag into each page you create.

Meta Author Tag Example

Most people who use this Meta Tag simply use:

<META name="Author" content="Webmaster (webmaster@exampledomain.com).">

Note that webmaster@exampledomain.com used in the above example should be your email address and 'Webmaster' should be the title or your name,you, or that of your webmaster.

Meta Copyright Tag

The Meta Copyright Tag defines copyright information about your webpage.

This Meta Tag is not used or generally stored by most search engines; however, you should include this Meta Tag on each page you create to protect your work against plagiarism. On the internet, this guarantees you nothing, however it may prove useful in legal cases. The copyright Meta Tag defines any copyright statement you wish to disclose about your webpage. This statement can include trademark names, patent numbers, copyright or other information which you want to publicly disclose as your intellectual property.

How to use this Meta Tag

META Name: "Copyright"
General Usage: <META name="Copyright" content="Copyright Statement">

How Search Engines Use This Meta Tag

Generally, search engines do not read and/or store this information. For the purposes of raising your search engine rankings, this Meta Tag will not help you at all.

Meta Copyright Tag Example

Most people who use this Meta Tag simply use:

<META name="Copyright" content="Copyright © 2007 Samuel Blankson. All rights reserved.">

Meta Distribution Meta Tag

The Meta Distribution Tag defines the level of distribution of your webpage. This tag currently supports only three forms, Global (indicates that your webpage is intended for mass distribution to everyone), Local (intended for local distribution of your webpage), and IU - Internal Use (not intended for public distribution). The Meta Distribution Tag will in no way aid you improve your search engine rankings (unless you define it with IU, in which case it may further lower your chances of being seen at all).

How to use this Meta Tag

META Name:	"Distribution"
Supported Distributions:	Global | Local | IU
General Usage:	<META name="Distribution" content="Global">
	Note: Only use one of the above

How Search Engines Use This Meta Tag

This tag is ignored by all but a handful of search engines. Most search engines determine how to distribute your webpage through other means. If you do not want your pages distributed, simply use a better supported Meta Tag to restrict indexing of your webpage. We will cover this shortly.

Meta Distribution Tag Example

Most people who use this Meta Tag simply use:

<META name="Distribution" content="Global">

Meta Revisit-After Tag

The Meta Revisit-After Tag defines how many days the search engine should wait before revisiting your webpage. This is useful for pages that change frequently. It ensures that the search engine always indexes the latest page.

How to use this Meta Tag

META Name: "Revisit-After"
General   <META name="Revisit-After" content="X
Usage: Days">
              Note: X indicates a number

The Meta Revisit-After Tag is widely supported and thus, can be beneficial for use to boost your search engine rankings. The sad thing is that Google has never supported this Meta Tag. However, plenty of other search engines do support it. Therefore, you can use it most effectively with the search engines amongst these that list search results based on the most recent submissions. Make sure your pages' content changes with each revisit. This way the search engine's spider programs will keep revisiting your webpage's.

How Search Engines Use This Meta Tag

The Meta Revisit-After Tag is used by most search engines to determine the revisit date for re-indexing of your webpage.

Meta Revisit-After Tag Example

<META name="Revisit-After" content="2 Days">

Meta Expires Tag

The Meta Expires Tag defines the expiry date of your webpage. This thus stops the page being indexed, and tells the search engines to delete the page from their database when it expires. This is a useful feature for use with time sensitive web pages.

The Meta Expires Tag is commonly used in conjunction with the Meta Revisit-After Tag as a means to get search engines to re-visit a website every few days. This is commonly used by websites who update their content frequently and want search engines to have a fresh copy of their content or webmasters wanting to improve their rankings through adding dynamically changing content. This need justifies web pages requiring frequent indexing. Also note that search engines that list search results based on submissions will raise their rankings for pages that are frequently submitted in this way.

How to use this Meta Tag

META Name: "Expires"
General Usage: <META name="Expires" content="Tue, 01
                 Jun 1999 19:58:02 GMT">
Note: Requires RFC1123 date as shown above
HTTP Header: Expires: Tue, 01 Jun 1999 19:58:02 GMT

On some search engines a value of "0" signifies immediately.

Meta Expires Tag Example

<META name="Expires" content="Sun, 01 Apr 2007 23:59:00 GMT">

Meta Content-Language Tag

The Meta Content-Language Tag defines the language used on your webpage. Some search engines index web pages based on supported languages. For English websites, this tag is not so useful; however, for non-English and multilingual websites; this Meta Tag is very useful. It allows correct indexing of the sites – according to the webpage's language. All RFC1766 languages are supported.

How to use this Meta Tag

HTTP-EQUIV:	"Content-Language"
Supported	All RFC1766 compliant languages
Languages	including the following:
	BG (Bulgarian)
	CS (Czech)
	DA (Danish)
	DE (German)
	EL (Greek)
	EN (English)
	EN-GB (English-Great Britain)
	EN-US (English-United States)
	ES (Spanish)
	ES-ES (Spanish-Spain)
	FI (Finnish)
	HR (Croatian)
	IT (Italian)
	FR (French)
	FR-CA (French-Quebec)
	FR-FR (French-France)
	IT (Italian)
	JA (Japanese)
	KO (Korean)
	NL (Dutch)
	NO (Norwegian)

	PL (Polish)
	PT (Portuguese)
	RU (Russian)
	SV (Swedish)
	ZH (Chinese)
General Usage:	*<META HTTP-EQUIV="Content-Language" content="EN">*
HTTP Header:	*Content-Language: EN*

Languages can also be specified as pairs, i.e. EN-GB for English-British.

To allow search engines that support this Meta Tag to index your site in the correct language, it is useful to define the language using the Meta Content-Language Tag.

How Search Engines Use This Meta Tag

The Language Meta Tag is not used very often by search engines; although, if your web page is not in English or has more than one language – as previously said – you may want to use this Meta Tag to indicate to search engines that your site is multi-lingual and to indicate which languages your webpage supports.

Meta Expires Tag Example

The most common usage of this Meta Tag is:

<META HTTP-EQUIV="Content-Language" content="EN-US">

HTTP Header Example

Content-Language: EN-US

Meta Refresh Tag

The Refresh Tag defines the number of seconds to wait before your webpage should be refreshed. This Meta Tag is useful when redirecting visitors to another page. It allows you to specify a time delay in seconds to wait before redirecting.

Most search engines do not like this feature as it can be used to SPAM search engines by using pages that reference other pages in an unending loop. The Meta Refresh Tag also leads to duplication in search engine databases due to multiple pages pointing to the same page.

Do not use scripts that reload a webpage whilst you also use the Meta Refresh Tag. Doing so could cause unwanted behavior or leave the Meta Tag undefined.

How to use this Meta Tag

META HTTP-EQUIV:	"Refresh"
General Usage:	<META HTTP-EQUIV="Refresh" content="X;URL=http://www.website.com/index.html"> Note: X indicates delay in seconds URL indicates the URL to redirect to
HTTP Header	Refresh: X;URL=http://www.website.com/index.html

How Search Engines Use This Meta Tag

Avoid using the Meta Refresh Tag on pages that you submit to search engines as most search engines have protective algorithms to detect and ignore pages that contain this Meta Tag; or worse, they may ban your site or host completely. If you must use Meta Refresh Tags on your web pages, make sure you also use the Meta

Robots Tag to switch off the indexing of the pages in which you are using the Meta Refresh Tag.

Meta Expires Tag Example

<META HTTP-EQUIV="Refresh"
content="3;URL=http://www.samuelblankson.com/index.html"
>

HTTP Header Example

Refresh: 3;URL=http://www.samuelblankson.com/index.html

Meta Page-Enter, Meta Page-Exit, Meta Site-Enter, Meta Site-Exit Tags

The Meta Page-Enter, Meta Page-Exit, Meta Site-Enter, and Meta Site-Exit Tags define special transition effects when opening or exiting a site or webpage.

How to use this Meta Tag

META HTTP-EQUIV:	"Page-Enter" | "Page-Exit" | "Site-Enter" | "Site-Exit"
General Usage:	<META HTTP EQUIV="Page-Enter" | "Page-Exit" | "Site-Enter" | "Site-Exit" content="effect(Duration=x,Transition=y)">
HTTP Header	Page-Enter | Page-Exit | Site-Enter | Site-Exit: effect(Duration=x,Transition=y)

This Meta Tag will not help your ranking on search engines.

Window-Target Tag Example
< META HTTP EQUIV="Page-Enter"
content="revealTrans(Duration=3.0,Transition=2)">

HTTP Header Example
Page-Enter: revealTrans(Duration=3.0,Transition=2)

Meta Googlebot Tag

The Meta Googlebot Tag is only supported by Google. It controls archiving, excerpt display, caching, indexing and 'spidering' of your web pages by the Google robots.

How to use this Meta Tag

META NAME: "Googlebot"

General Usage: meta name= "googlebot" CONTENT="noarchive" | "nosnippet" | "noindex" | "nofollow">

HTTP Header   Googlebot: noarchive | nosnippet | noindex | nofollow

The following are the Googlebot elements:

- googlebot: noarchive (do not allow Google to display cached content)
- googlebot: nosnippet (do not allow Google to display excerpt or cached content)
- googlebot: noindex (do not index, similar to the robots meta element)
- googlebot: nofollow (do not traverse linked pages, similar to the robots meta element)

This Meta Tag will help you control what Google does with your web pages but it won't help your search engine ranking, especially outside Google.

Window-Target Tag Examples

<meta name= "googlebot" CONTENT="noarchive">
<meta name= "googlebot" CONTENT="nosnippet">
<meta name= "googlebot" CONTENT="noindex">
<meta name= "googlebot" CONTENT="nofollow">

HTTP Header Example

Googlebot: noarchive
Googlebot: nosnippet
Googlebot: noindex
Googlebot: nofollow

Meta Content-Disposition Tag

This Meta Tag specifies an application handler. It helps associate applications with content types. Typically, you must specify a content-type before you specify the Meta Content-Disposition Tag. It will not help you with search engine rankings but may help your web content be viewed by various browsers.

How to use this Meta Tag

META HTTP-EQUIV:	"Content-Disposition"
General Usage:	<META HTTP-EQUIV="Content-Disposition" content="disposition type; disposition parameter">
HTTP Header	Content-Disposition: disposition type; disposition-parameter"

This Meta Tag will not help your rankings on search engines.

The disposition-type can either be inline or attachment.
You can use the following disposition-parameters:
- filename-parm := "filename" "=" value
- creation-date-parm := "creation-date" "=" quoted-date-time
- modification-date-parm := "modification-date" "=" quoted-date-time
- read-date-parm := "read-date" "=" quoted-date-time
- size-parm := "size" "=" 1*DIGIT
- quoted-date-time := quoted-string
  (Contents MUST be an RFC 822 `date-time numeric timezones (+HHMM or -HHMM) MUST be used)

Meta Content-Disposition Tag Example

<META HTTP-EQUIV="Content-Type"
CONTENT="text/comma-separated-values">
<META HTTP-EQUIV="Content-Disposition"
CONTENT="inline; filename=openinexcel.csv">

HTTP Header Example

Content-Type: text/comma-separated-values
Content-Disposition: inline; filename=openinexcel.csv

Meta Imagetoolbar Tag

The Meta Imagetoolbar Tag is mainly used to control the toolbar displayed on images viewed through Internet Explorer. To allow the images to be displayed, simply don't use this Meta Tag. To stop the toolbars being displayed, use these Meta Tag.

How to use this Meta Tag

META HTTP-EQUIV:	"imagetoolbar"
General Usage:	<META HTTP-EQUIV="imagetoolbar" CONTENT="yes | no">
HTTP Header	Imagetoolbar: yes | no

This Meta Tag does not help with search engine ranking; it simply offers aesthetic assistance with a few web browsers.

Meta Content-Disposition Tag Example

<META HTTP-EQUIV="imagetoolbar" CONTENT="no">

HTTP Header Example

imagetoolbar: no

Meta Pragma Tag

The Meta Pragma Tag is hardly supported anymore. Internet Explorer for instance stopped supporting it from IE5. It controls caching through the no-cache value. This Meta Tag stops local caching of a web page. It can be useful for keeping secure pages un-cached.

How to use this Meta Tag

META HTTP-EQUIV:	"Pragma"
General Usage:	<META HTTP-EQUIV="Pragma" content="value">
HTTP Header	Pragma: value

This Meta Tag does not help with search engine ranking.

Meta Content-Disposition Tag Example
<META HTTP-EQUIV="Pragma" CONTENT="no-cache">

HTTP Header Example
Pragma: no-cache

Meta Content-Type Tag

The Meta Content-Type defines the content type of the document or webpage. It can be extended to include the character set. It is recommended that you always use this to ensure your webpage is displayed correctly in cases where your document may be displayed in an incorrect character set.

How to use this Meta Tag

META HTTP-EQUIV:	"Content-Type"
General Usage:	<META HTTP-EQUIV="Content-Type" CONTENT="doc-type; doc-parameter">
HTTP Header	Content-Type: doc-type; doc-parameter ">

This Meta Tag will not help your rankings on search engines.

Meta Content-Type Tag Example

<META HTTP-EQUIV="Content-Type" CONTENT=" text/html; charset ISO-8859-1">

HTTP Header Example

Content-Type: text/html; charset ISO-8859-1

Meta Content-Script-Type Tag

The Meta Content-Script-Type specifies the default scripting language in a document.

How to use this Meta Tag

META HTTP-EQUIV:	"Content-Script-Type"
General Usage:	<META HTTP-EQUIV=" Content-Script-Type" content="text/javascript">
HTTP Header	Resource-Type: text/javascript

This Meta Tag will not help your search engine rankings.

This Meta Tag uses Mimetypes for applicable values.

List of Mimetypes

The Mimetypes consist of a content type and a subtype i.e. text/plain. The following are a listing of the main mime types:

- *text/plain* - text with no special formatting requirements.
- text/html - text with embedded HTML commands
- *application/binary* - the data is in some unknown binary format, such as the results of a file transfer.
- *application/postscript* - the data is in the postscript language, and should be fed to a postscript interpreter.
- *image/gif* - an image in the GIF format.
- *image/xbm* - an image in the X Bitmap format.
- *image/jpeg* - an image in the JPEG format.
- *audio/basic* - the data consists of 8 KHz 8 bit mu-law audio samples. This is the standard way that audio is encoded digitally for the telephone system in the US and Japan, and because of this, many inexpensive hardware devices exist now on computers for input and output in this form. Basically, the analog audio is sampled in 8 bit chunks 8000

times a second, and each chunk assigned a "pulse" value. mu-law refers to the way the "sound" of the pulse is converted to an 8 bit values.

- *video/mpeg* - the data is MPEG format video
- *video/QuickTime* - the data is QuickTime format video

Meta Content-Script-Type Tag Example

<META HTTP-EQUIV="Content-Script-Type"
CONTENT="text/javascript">

HTTP Header Example

Content-Script-Type: text/javascript

Meta Content-Style-Type Tag

The Meta Content-Style-Type specifies the default style sheet for a document.

How to use this Meta Tag

META HTTP-EQUIV: "Content-Script-Type"
General Usage: <META HTTP-EQUIV="Content-Style-Type" CONTENT="text/css">
HTTP Header   Content-Style-Type: text/css

This Meta Tag will not help your search engine rankings.

Content-Style-Type Tag Example

<META HTTP-EQUIV="Content-Style-Type" CONTENT="text/css">

HTTP Header Example

Content-Style-Type: text/css

Meta Default-Style Tag

The Meta Default-Style Tag sets the documents preferred style sheet. This is taken from a style sheet specified elsewhere through a LINK element.

How to use this Meta Tag

META HTTP-EQUIV: "Default-Style"
General Usage: <META HTTP-EQUIV="Default-Style" CONTENT="style-value">
HTTP Header   Default-Style: style-value

This Meta Tag will not help your search engine rankings.

Default-Style Tag Example

<META HTTP-EQUIV="Default-Style"
CONTENT="compact">

HTTP Header Example

Default-Style: compact

Meta Window-target Tag

The Meta Window-Target Tag specifies the named window of the current page. It can stop many browsers from displaying a page in a frame.

How to use this Meta Tag

META HTTP-EQUIV: "Window-Target"

General Usage: <META HTTP-EQUIV="Window-target" CONTENT="value">

HTTP Header   Window-target: value

This Meta Tag will not help your search engine rankings.

Window-Target Tag Example

<META HTTP-EQUIV="Window-target" CONTENT="_top">

HTTP Header Example

Window-target: _top

Meta Ext-Cache Tag

The Meta Ext-Cache Tag defines the name of an alternate cache. This Meta Tag was introduced and supported by Netscape browsers but is hardly used by others.

How to use this Meta Tag

META HTTP-EQUIV:	"Ext-Cache"
General Usage:	<META HTTP-EQUIV="Ext-cache" CONTENT="name= database-path; instructions=User Instructions">
HTTP Header	Ext-cache: name=database-path; instructions=User Instructions">

This Meta Tag will not help your search engine rankings.

Ext-Cache Tag Example

<META HTTP-EQUIV="Ext-cache"
CONTENT="name=/some/path/index.db; instructions=User Instructions">

HTTP Header Example

Ext-cache: name=/some/path/index.db; instructions=User Instructions">

Set-Cookie Tag

The Meta Set-Cookie Tag was introduced by Netscape and it sets a "cookie" in the browser. Values with an expiry date are considered "permanent" and will be saved to disk on exit, whilst those without will not be saved to disk on exit.

How to use this Meta Tag

META HTTP-EQUIV:	"Set-Cookie"
General Usage:	<META HTTP-EQUIV="Set-Cookie" CONTENT="cookievalue=cookie-name;expires=expiry-time-date; path=/">
HTTP Header	Set-Cookie: cookievalue=cookie-name;expires=expiry-time-date; path=/

This Meta Tag will not help your search engine rankings.

Set-Cookie Tag Example

<META HTTP-EQUIV="Set-Cookie"
CONTENT="cookievalue=xxx;expires=Friday, 31-Dec-08
23:59:59 GMT; path=/">

HTTP Header Example

Set-Cookie: cookievalue=xxx;expires=Friday, 31-Dec-08
23:59:59 GMT; path=/

Meta Cache-Control Tag

The Meta Cache-Control Tag specifies the action of cache agents. Possible values are:

- Public - may be cached in public shared caches.
- Private - may only be cached in private cache.
- no-cache - may not be cached.
- no-store - may be cached but not archived.

Note that whilst using these headers as META tags, browser action is undefined.

How to use this Meta Tag

META HTTP-EQUIV:	"Cache-Control"
General Usage:	<META HTTP-EQUIV="Cache-Control" CONTENT="Public | Private | no-cache | no-store">
	Cache-Control: Public | Private | no-cache | no-store
HTTP Header	

This Meta Tag will not help your search engine rankings.

Cache-Control Tag Example

<META HTTP-EQUIV="Cache-Control"
CONTENT="public">

HTTP Header Example

Cache-Control: public

Meta Vary Tag

The Meta Vary Tag specifies that alternates are available.

How to use this Meta Tag

META HTTP-EQUIV: "Vary"
General Usage: <META HTTP-EQUIV="Vary"
                               CONTENT="Content-language">
                               Vary: Content-language

HTTP Header

This Meta Tag will not help your search engine rankings.

It simply allows alternatives to be used wherever they are available in the specified value. In the above example "Vary: Content-language" implies that if a header Accept-Language is sent, an alternate form may be selected.

Window-Target Tag Example

<META HTTP-EQUIV="Vary" CONTENT="Content-language">

HTTP Header Example

Vary: Content-language

Meta PICS-Label Tag

The Meta PICS-Label Tag is a highly flexible Platform-Independent Content rating Scheme (PICS). Typically used to declare a document's rating in terms of the following categories:

Category: Multiculturalism

Description: Representation of multi-cultural activity or activities from another culture.

- **Interactive:** Active involvement of user in multicultural activity using interactive techniques.
- **Promotion:** Active promotion of multiculturalism.
- **Positive:** Multicultural events presented in context; artistic work presented in the original culture.
- **Neutral:** No cultural context; reference works, dictionaries, catalogs.
- **Negative:** Multicultural events presented from a monoculture viewpoint; translation of artistic work from one culture into another for other than artistic reasons.
- **Demotion:** Actively discourages multiculturalism; one culture or religion is defined as the only true culture.

Category: Educational Content

- **Interactive:** Active involvement of user in educational activity using interactive techniques.
- **Educational:** Educational material, created specifically to educate.
- **Informative:** Informational material, dictionaries, catalogs, factual accounts, works of literature, works of art, etc.
- **None:** Devoid of educational or artistic content.
- **Misinformation:** Presents information known to be false as fact; e.g. Holocaust denial.

Category: Environmental Awareness

- **Interactive:** Active involvement of user in environmentally positive activity using interactive techniques.
- **Promotion:** Encouragement of environmental awareness.
- **Positive:** Portrayal of environmentally sensitive behavior; recycling, conservation, proper disposal etc.
- **Neutral:** No environmental content.
- **Negative:** Portrayal of environmentally insensitive behavior by minor characters; pollution of resources, improper disposal.
- **Demotion:** Promotion of environmentally damaging behavior by role-model figures; destruction of resources, habitat, animal species.

Category: Tolerance

- **Promotion:** Promotion of tolerant behavior.
- **Positive:** Portrayal of tolerant behavior.
- **Neutral:** No Intolerant content; reference works, etc.
- **Negative:** Portrayal of intolerant behavior by minor characters.
- **Intolerance:** Portrayal of intolerant behavior by role-model figures.
- **Active Intolerance:** Promoting hatred based on differences in religion, culture, race, sexual orientation etc.
- **Unlimited Intolerance:** Active promotion of intolerant behavior; calling for ethnic cleansing, Jihad, genocide etc.

Category: Violence

- **None:** No violent content.
- **Reference:** Reference works portraying violence, news with violent content.
- **Minor:** In-context violence by minor characters, self-defense by role models.
- **Major:** In-context violence by role model characters.

- **Extreme:** Frequent violence by role models, promotion of violent behavior, treatment of human beings as disposable objects, rape.
- **Unlimited:** Killing, torture, rape in creation of entertainment product. Snuff movies. Active involvement of the user in violent activity using teleoperator techniques, remote controlled torture of animals or humans.

Category: Sex

- **None:** No sexual content.
- **Minor:** Implicit in-context sexual conduct by consenting adults; no nudity.
- **Reference:** Reference works portraying sex, reproduction; educational material.
- **Nudity:** In-context sexual conduct by consenting adults; nudity, no penetration. Out-of-context sexual conduct, partial nudity; sex used as a promotional tool.
- **Normal:** In-context sexual conduct by consenting adults; vaginal penetration of female by male only.
- **Other:** Sexual conduct by consenting adults; penetration, anal, toys. Interactive viewing of sexual activity using videoconference techniques.
- **Interactive:** Active involvement of the user in sexual activity using teleoperator techniques, tactile virtual reality.
- **Unlimited:** Non-consensual sex, rape, sex with minors, animals; mutilation, torture.

Category: Profanity

- **None:** No profanity.
- **Reference:** Reference works, dictionaries.
- **Minor:** Occasional profanity by minor characters; mild in-context profanity by role model characters.
- **Major:** Frequent profanity by role model characters.
- **Unlimited:** Constant profanity by all characters.

Category: Safety

Description: Treatment of personal and general safety issues

- **Active:** Active promotion of safe work and personal behavior.
- **Positive:** Portrayal of safe behavior by role-models. Technical manuals and books describing safe practice.
- **Neutral:** No safety-related content.
- **Negative:** Promotion of unsafe behavior. Drug use, reckless driving by role models. Suggestions that safe behavior is effeminate or unmanly.
- **Misleading:** Presentation of misleading information that if acted on could result in injury or death. Representation of known harmful activities such as smoking as beneficial.

Category: Canadian Content

- **All:** All-Canadian content
- **Some:** Some Canadian content or production
- **None:** No Canadian content

Category: Commercial Content

- **None:** No commercial content; no advertising material.
- **Minor:** Minor commercial content, corporate sponsorship, low-key advertising.
- **Major:** Major commercial content, high-impact advertising, infomercials
- **Interactive:** Online purchasing of products or services.

Category: Gambling

- **None:** No gambling or games of chance.
- **Fun:** Games of chance for fun only; no monetary value of stakes or prizes.
- **No-stake:** Limited games of chance, no monetary value of stakes.

- **Unlimited:** Games of chance where stakes must be purchased or have a monetary value.

How to use this Meta Tag

META HTTP-EQUIV: "PICS-Label"

General Usage: <META http-equiv="PICS-Label" content='(PICS-1.1"Website of service provider" l gen true comment "location on server" by "rater email or website address" on "time and date" for "requester email or website address" r (Gam 0 V 0 Env 0 SF 0 Com 0 Can 0 Edu 0 S 0 P 0 Tol 0 MC 0))'>

HTTP Header   PICS-Label: <META http-equiv="PICS-Label" content='(PICS-1.1"Website of service provider" l gen true comment "location on server" by "rater email or website address" on "time and date" for "requester email or website address" r (Gam 0 V 0 Env 0 SF 0 Com 0 Can 0 Edu 0 S 0 P 0 Tol 0 MC 0))'>

This Meta Tag will not help your search engine
rankings.

PICS-Label Tag Example

<META http-equiv="PICS-Label" content='(PICS-
1.1"http://vancouver-webpages.com/VWP1.0/" l gen true
comment "VWP1.0" by "http://www.samuelblankson.com" on
"2007.03.20T18:001700" for
"http://www.samuelblankson.com" r (Gam 0 V 0 Env 0 SF 0
Com 0 Can 0 Edu 0 S 0 P 0 Tol 0 MC 0))'>

HTTP Header Example

PICS-Label: (PICS-1.1 "http://vancouver-
webpages.com/VWP1.0/" l gen true by
"http://www.samuelblankson.com" on "2007.03.20T18:001700"
for "http://www.samuelblankson.com" r (Gam 0 V 0 Env 0 SF 0
Com 0 Can 0 Edu 0 S 0 P 0 Tol 0 MC 0))

Meta Msthemecopmpatible Tag

The Meta Msthemecompatible Tag disables theming support for the document. Microsoft introduced this tag for Internet Explorer.

How to use this Meta Tag

META NAME:	"Msthemecompatible"
General Usage:	<META HTTP-EQUIV="MSThemeCompatible" Content="no">
HTTP Header	MSThemeCompatible: "no"

This Meta Tag will not help your search engine rankings.

When running on Windows XP and Internet Explorer 6, the content displayed has a look and feel that matches the Windows XP platform. This Meta Tag allows you to switch this feature off.

Window-Target Tag Example

<META HTTP-EQUIV="MSThemeCompatible" Content="no">

HTTP Header Example

MSThemeCompatible: no

Meta No-Email-Collection Tag

The Meta No-Email-Collection Tag is an initiative of unspam.com. It aims to put an end to email address harvesting by compliant robots.

How to use this Meta Tag

META NAME: "no-email-collection"

General Usage: <meta name="no-email-collection" Content="[link to your terms]"/>

You can either replace the [link to your terms] with a link to your terms of use page or link it to www.unspam.com/noemailcollection

This Meta Tag will not help your search engine rankings.

Window-Target Tag Example

<Meta NAME="no-email-collection" value="http://www.unspam.com/noemailcollection"/>

Meta Robots Tag

The Meta Robots Tag declares to search engines what content to index and spider.

Typically, a website owner would submit the main page and the robots would visit your site and collect all sub-pages and related links from your main page. Robots, also known as spiders, are automated programs that spider your site, or search your site on how to categorize the information you submitted to the search engine.

However, the Meta Robots Tag enables you to control which pages you would like spidered, and which to ignore. For instance, you may not want certain web pages and directories (i.e. password folders or CGI Scripts) indexed in the search engines. Using the Meta Robots Tag, you can define which pages to follow, which to index and which to ignore completely.

In practice, search engine robots follow all links in your website by default; therefore, you do not need to use the Meta Robots Tag to force them to do this; however, where this Meta Tag is most utilized is in stopping robots from spidering certain pages.

You can also use a file called robots.txt (must be all lowercase) placed in the root of your website to achieve the same objective. You do not need to use both conventions – use either the robots.txt or the Meta Robots Tag.

How to use this Meta Tag

META Name: "Robots"
Supported Types: all | none | noindex | index | nofollow | follow | noimageindex | noimageclick
General Usage: <META name="Robots" content="index,follow ">

This is a well-supported Meta Tag and is supported by most of the larger search engines. As an example, AltaVista for instance who supports the following types:

- *NOINDEX* - prevents anything on the page from being indexed.
- *NOFOLLOW* - prevents the robot from following the links on the page and indexing the linked pages.
- *NOIMAGEINDEX* - prevents the images on the page from being indexed but the text on the page can still be indexed.
- *NOIMAGECLICK* - prevents the use of links directly to the images, instead there will only be a link to the page.

The default is to index and follow all links if none of the above are defined in the Meta Robots Tag.

Using the Robots.txt convention

In 1993 and 1994 rogue robot activities forced a mechanism to be developed to tackle robots that traversed through sections of a website they shouldn't have. These viruses and other robots caused all sorts of havoc, from affecting web votes to actually bringing web servers and mail servers down by swamping web servers with multiple page requests. The robots.txt file mechanism was devised to tackle this issue.

You can use a file called robot.txt placed in the root of your website to control the robots that visit your site. To do this you must follow the following format in the robots.txt file:

- There must only be one robots.txt file per website.
- The robots.txt file must be placed in the root of your website, not inside any subfolders, i.e. http://www.practicalbooks.org/robots.txt, http://www. practicalbooks.org:80/robots.txt, http://www.

practicalbooks.org:1234/robots.txt or http://
practicalbooks.org/robots.txt.

- The robots.txt file must be called robots.txt and not Robots.txt or any other variation in the case or spelling.
- The robots.txt file must contain the following format:
  - User-agent: * *{User-agent: * means all robots, whilst User-agent: WebCrawler for instance, would apply only to the WebCrawler robots.}*
  - Disallow: / *{for blocking i.e. Disallow: /tmp/} or Disallow: {for allowing i.e. Disallow: tmp. The / controls blocking whilst Disallow: means allow all.}*
- Each Disallow: must be on a separate line.
- There must not be any blank lines.
- The '*' in the User-agent field is a special value meaning "any robot". You cannot use * to mean anything else on other lines.
- To allow all robots to index all of your site, use a blank robot.txt file or the following:

        User-agent: *
        Disallow:

- To exclude all robots from indexing all of your website, use the following:

        User-agent: *
        Disallow: /

- To exclude all robots from certain folders (i.e. cgi-bin, tmp or password), use the following:

        User-agent: *
        Disallow: /cgi-bin
        Disallow: /tmp
        Disallow: /password

Note that using the above without a '/' symbol on the end of the Disallow: instruction will block all contents of that folder. To only act on the index.html in a folder, place a / symbol at the end of the Disallow: instruction as follows:

        User-agent: *
        Disallow: /cgi-bin/

Disallow: /tmp/
Disallow: /password/

- To exclude a single robot (i.e. WebCrawler) from indexing your site, use the following:

    User-agent: WebCrawler
    Disallow: /

- To allow only a single robot, you must first allow that robot then block all others.

    User-agent: WebCrawler
    Disallow:
    User-agent: *
    Disallow: /

- To exclude all but one file, you must either move all files you wish to block into a folder and leave the single file to allow outside that folder (you can then block the folder with all the files you wish to block using the following:

    User-agent: *
    Disallow: /personal/hide/

    or exclude all files except the one you wish to allow as in the following example:

    User-agent: *
    Disallow: /personal/file1.html
    Disallow: /personal/file2.html
    Disallow: /personal/filex.html

If you use robots.txt, you need not also use the Meta Robots Tag.

How Search Engines Use This Meta Tag

The Robots Meta Tag and robots.txt convention is used by search engines as a means to indicate the level of spidering a search engine should do. Most search engines look for this Meta Tag and will only index and/or spider the pages you want to be indexed.

Meta Expires Tag Example

```
<meta name="robots" content="all">
<meta name="robots" content="none">
<meta name="robots" content="index,follow">
<meta name="robots" content="noindex,follow">
<meta name="robots" content="index,nofollow">
<meta name="robots" content="noindex,nofollow">
```

The Meta Keywords Tag

The Meta Keywords Tag allows you to provide additional text for search engines to index along with your body text, and used to be well supported by six out of the top ten search engines in 1997, however; nowadays it is not supported by major search engines since Inktomi, its last remaining supporter was bought by Yahoo! in 2002.

The reason for the drop in the Meta Keywords Tag's popularity lies in the simple fact that it can be too easily abused by spammers. Simply by repeating keywords and including keywords that covered all possibilities of a search in a particular category(s), webmasters were able to easily and effortlessly raise their search engine site ranking – for free.

There continues to be a few smaller search engines still supporting this Meta Tag; however the effort to include and update it for the results you will achieve may be counter productive.

How to use this Meta Tag

META NAME: "Keywords"
General Usage: <meta name="keywords" content="list your keywords separated by commas"/>

Many smaller search engines still support the Meta Keyword Tag and so it may still be worth using on your web pages. To use it, simply use a keyword suggestion tool to find the most relevant keywords for your site/page. Then rewrite your site body text to include these keywords. Once you have included these keywords within your page/site body text, you can then include them in the Meta Keyword Tag.

This is not the only use the Meta Keyword Tag has however; it can also help in including synonyms or unusual words that don't appear on the page itself. As an example, if your page was all about tables but your text never mentions tennis, then placing Tennis in your Meta Keyword Tag may help your page be included in searches for "Table Tennis", and "Tennis Table".

However, an obvious fact stands out here, your page would fair even better in searches for "Table tennis" if you actually included the word in your webpage/website body text. The same goes for keywords that are used together, hyphenated or separated, i.e. "space-time", "space time" or "spacetime". In the case of space and time, you would make sure you included all three representations within your body text and Meta Keywords Tag.

The last major search engine, to drop this Meta Tag, Inktomi, advised webmasters to include up to 25 words or phrases separated by commas in the Meta Keywords Tag. The search engines that support keyword tags generally have a cutoff point of a thousand characters that they index, therefore writing longer keyword lists is probably counterproductive. Excessive repetitions of keywords or phrases will likely get your page, site or domain banned; therefore avoid doing this.

Keywords Tag Example

<META NAME="keywords"CONTENT="book,books,blankson,samuel, samuel blankson,meta tags,meta tag,metatag,metatags, seo,s.e.o.,search engine optimization,rankings,ranking,search engine,page rank,keyword tag,keywords tag,keyword tags">

Meta Rating Tag

The Meta Rating Tag allows website owners to self-rate their websites' appropriateness for the younger web audience.

The Meta Rating Tag is used to give the web page a rating for the appropriateness for children. The ratings are, general, mature, restricted, and 14 years.

How to use this Meta Tag

META Name: "Rating"
Supported Types: general | mature | restricted | 14 years
General Usage: <META name="Rating" content="general">

How Search Engines Use This Meta Tag

Most search engines don't look for this Meta Tag and will generate their own rating from the title and content of the sites pages.

Meta Ratings Tag Example

<META name="Rating" content="general">

Meta Resource-Type Tag

The Meta Resource-Type Meta Tag defines a resource. This helps cataloging of resources available on your website.

Using the Meta Resource-Type Tag is not going to get you ranked higher by the major search engines; however, it will help you maintain a well organized and catalogued website. This feature is particularly useful for academic and data warehouse websites.

How to use this Meta Tag

META HTTP-EQUIV:	"Resource-Type"
General Usage:	<META HTTP-EQUIV="Resource-Type" content="document">
HTTP Header	Resource-Type: document

Meta Ratings Tag Example

<META content="document">	HTTP-EQUIV="Resource-Type"

HTTP Header Example
Resource-Type: document

Other Meta Tags

There are many other Meta Tags that exist beyond those explored in this book. For example, websites can use a wide variety of Meta Tags for internal use. These Meta Tags will not be supported or understood by search engines outside the internal network; and in fact, they do not need to be if their sole purpose is for internal private use. As the main search engines would not use or understand these internal Meta Tags I have not covered them all in this book.

A new initiative that is currently poorly supported but holds a lot of promise is the "Dublin Core" Meta Tags. Dublin Core addresses the internal external use issue by providing a range of Meta Tags that could be used both internally in private networks, and externally on the public internet domain. For more information on the Dublin Core Meta Tags, visit http://dublincore.org.

Dublin Core

DC.TITLE
DC.CREATOR
DC.SUBJECT
DC.DESCRIPTION
DC.PUBLISHER
DC.CONTRIBUTORS
DC.DATE
DC.TYPE
DC.FORMAT
DC.IDENTIFIER
DC.SOURCE
DC.LANGUAGE
DC.RELATION
DC.COVERAGE
DC.RIGHTS

The Dublin Core initiative introduces a formal approach in an attempt to unify and standardize all other Meta Tag elements. The Dublin Core Meta Tags can be reused as many times as you wish without limit. The Meta Tags are preceded with DC and the standard is flexible enough to be applied to any resource or information as well as having possibilities for a broader application.

The standard for describing data elements is the ISO/IEC 11179. Dublin Core uses ten attributes from ISO/IEC 11179 to describe the DC Elements. These include:

- **Name** - The name assigned to the data element.
- **Identifier** - The unique identifier assigned to the data element.
- **Version** - The version of the data element.
- **Registration Authority** - The person/company/service authorized to register the data element.
- **Language** - The language in which the data element is specified.
- **Definition** – A definition of the data element.
- **Obligation** – This indicates if the data element is required to always or sometimes contain a value.
- **Data type** – The type of data that can be represented in the value of the data element.
- **Maximum Occurrence** - Indicates how many times the data element can be repeated.
- **Comment** – Any extra comments relating to the application of the data element.

The above list contributes to the formal definition of the Dublin Core Meta Tags.

How to use Dublin Core Meta Tags

META NAME: "DC.Identifier"
General Usage: <META NAME="DC.Identifier"
                  CONTENT="(SCHEME=URL) URL web
                  address">
                  <LINK REL=SCHEMA.dc
                  HREF="http://purl.org/metadata/dublin_core_e
                  lements#name of element">

As the Dublin Core is not yet widely supported by the major search engines it will be fruitless to use it for improving your search engine rankings. However, if you want to use the elements, you are advised to define the schema with <LINK REL=SCHEMA.dc HREF="http://purl.org/metadata/dublin_core_elements# followed by the name of the identifier without the dc (see the example below for more information).

Window-Target Tag Example

<META NAME="DC.Identifier"
CONTENT="(SCHEME=URL) URL
http://www.samuelblankson.com">
<LINK REL=SCHEMA.dc
HREF="http://purl.org/metadata/dublin_core_elements#identifi
er">

Miscellaneous

There are loads of other Meta Tags that are no good for improving your search engine ranking; however, they allow you to improve your websites professionalism and make cataloguing and indexing by many other search engines easier. The following are a few of them and examples of their use:

Meta Version Tag

This allows you to specify a version identifier for your document.

Usage
<META NAME="version" content="S5 1.1">

Meta Generator Tag

This specifies what program generated the HTML of your webpage. This is normally automatically generated by the web authoring software.

Usage
<META NAME="generator" content=" [generating program] ">

Meta Presdate Tag

This allows you to specify the presentation date of your presentation document.

Usage
<META NAME="presdate" content=" [presentation date] ">

Meta Template Tag

This allows you to specify the location of the template document used to create the document.

Usage
<META NAME="Template" CONTENT="C:\Program Files\Microsoft Office\Office\html.dot">

Meta Operator Tag

This specifies the resource operator's name.

Usage
<META NAME="operator" content="Samuel Blankson">

Meta Creation Date Tag

This specifies the date of creation of the document.

Usage
<META NAME="creation_date" CONTENT="March 30, 2007 00:00:01">

Meta Host Tag

This specifies the address (normally a URL) of the page host site.

Usage
<META NAME="host" content="www.samuelblankson.com">

Meta Host-Admin Tag

Specifies the host site admin contact address (normally an email address).

Usage
```
<META NAME="host-admin"
content="info@samuelblankson.com">
```

Meta Classification Tag

Specifies what type of content is included in the document.

Usage
```
<META NAME="classification" content="data">
```

Meta Document-Type Tag

This specifies the type of document being displayed.

Usage
```
<META NAME="document-type" content="Web Page">
```

Meta Document-Rating Tag

See Meta Rating Tag.

Usage
```
<META NAME="document-rating" content="General">
```

Meta Document-Distribution, document-class Tag

See Meta Distribution Tag.

Usage
```
<META NAME="document-distribution" content="Global">
<META NAME="document-class" content="Global">
```

Meta Subject Tag

This specifies the webpage subject.

Usage
<META NAME="subject" CONTENT="Web Page Subject">

Meta Build Tag

This specifies the build identifier for the document or file.

Usage
<META NAME="build" CONTENT=" 2000.1.23 ">

Meta Location Tag

This specifies a geographic location.

Usage
<META NAME="location" CONTENT="WA,UK,Cardiff"

Meta Random Text Tags

You can make up your own special Meta Tags for internal use. These can be used with your private network or between other sites that support them.

Usage
Random Text (e.g., <META NAME="Samuel Blankson" Content="yes">)

Conclusion

Through the pages of this book, we have looked at Meta Tags in some detail. You will now know what the various Meta Tags are and how to use them to help you raise your visibility on the internet through search engines. You have also learned how you can use some Meta Tags to increase your webpage's professionalism and to aid search engines to better index your web pages.

In the last decade Google has risen to be the most popular and most used search engine in the world. As Google is not a big supporter of Meta Tags, Meta Tag usage and support has progressively declined. However, the majority of search engines still support many Meta Tags; therefore, learning to use these will greatly benefit your web site and web pages.

We have looked at how the Title Tag although not a true Meta Tag is used by almost all search engines (including Google), and therefore well worth using to assist your webpage's search rankings.

Meta Robots are another Meta Tag that enjoys full support by most search engines. However, only use it if you DO NOT want your pages indexed. Avoid using it to make your pages more visited as abuse of this tag could result in being banned or blacklisted by search engines.

The Meta Description Tag also enjoys much support, and it is well worth using. However, make sure you word your descriptions as follows:

1. Place the most important keywords in the first paragraph of your description
2. Keep it relevant to your content by making sure the description is well supported by the body text.

The Meta Keywords Tag is only supported by one search engine and probably isn't worth the time to implement. However, if you still want to use it, make sure you backup each keyword with an appearance in the body text of your webpage. Use synonyms abbreviations, Americanisms etc to support the main keywords from your body text in your Meta Keywords Tag.

And finally;finally, regularly carry out searches on the major search engines to see how your site or pages are doing. Examine your competitor's site/pages and HTML code for clues as to how they manage to be better ranked than you are. If you can apply the same techniques, Meta Tags or marketing to your site and pages without breaking copyright laws then do so. See Appendix 1 for further websites to explore for information on Meta tags.

Appendices

Appendix 1

Useful Websites

A Dictionary of HTML META Tags
http://vancouver-webpages.com/META/

Sun Microsystems Meta Tag guide
http://www.sun.com/webdesign/guidelines/metatags.html

W3Schools
http://www.w3schools.com/tags/tag_meta.asp

Dublin Core
http://dublincore.org/tools/
http://dublincore.org/documents/dcmi-terms/

Wikipedia
http://en.wikipedia.org/wiki/Meta_tag

W3
http://www.w3.org/TR/html401/struct/global.html

Software and web based generators
SiteUp's Meta-Tag Generator
http://www.siteup.com/meta.html

Free Meta Tags Builder
http://www.scrubtheweb.com/abs/builder.html

http://www.hisoftware.com/taggen.htm

http://www.ukoln.ac.uk/metadata/dcdot/

Meta Tag Builder
http://vancouver-webpages.com/META/mk-metas.html

Appendix 2

HTML 4.01 / XHTML 1.0 Reference

Ordered Alphabetically

- **NN**: indicates the earliest version of Netscape that supports the tag.
- **IE**: indicates the earliest version of Internet Explorer that supports the tag.
- **DTD**: indicates in which XHTML 1.0 DTD the tag is allowed. S=Strict, T=Transitional, and F=Frameset.

Tag	NN	IE	DTD	Description
<!--...-->	3.0	3.0	STF	*Defines a comment*
<!DOCTYPE>			STF	*Defines the document type*
<a>	3.0	3.0	STF	*Defines an anchor*
<abbr>	6.2		STF	*Defines an abbreviation*
<acronym>	6.2	4.0	STF	*Defines an acronym*
<address>	4.0	4.0	STF	*Defines an address element*
<applet>	2.0	3.0	TF	*Deprecated. Defines an applet*
<area>	3.0	3.0	STF	*Defines an area inside an image map*
<b>	3.0	3.0	STF	*Defines bold text*
<base>	3.0	3.0	STF	*Defines a base URL for all the links in a page*
<basefont>	3.0	3.0	TF	*Deprecated. Defines a base font*
<bdo>	6.2	5.0	STF	*Defines the direction of text display*
<big>	3.0	3.0	STF	*Defines big text*
<blockquote>	3.0	3.0	STF	*Defines a long quotation*
<body>	3.0	3.0	STF	*Defines the body element*
 	3.0	3.0	STF	*Inserts a single line break*
<button>	6.2	4.0	STF	*Defines a push button*
<caption>	3.0	3.0	STF	*Defines a table caption*
<center>	3.0	3.0	TF	*Deprecated. Defines centered text*
<cite>	3.0	3.0	STF	*Defines a citation*
<code>	3.0	3.0	STF	*Defines computer code text*
<col>		3.0	STF	*Defines attributes for table columns*
<colgroup>		3.0	STF	*Defines groups of table columns*
<dd>	3.0	3.0	STF	*Defines a definition description*
<del>	6.2	4.0	STF	*Defines deleted text*
<dir>	3.0	3.0	TF	*Deprecated. Defines a directory list*

<div>	3.0	3.0	STF	*Defines a section in a document*
<dfn>		3.0	STF	*Defines a definition term*
<dl>	3.0	3.0	STF	*Defines a definition list*
<dt>	3.0	3.0	STF	*Defines a definition term*
<em>	3.0	3.0	STF	*Defines emphasized text*
<fieldset>	6.2	4.0	STF	*Defines a fieldset*
<font>	3.0	3.0	TF	*Deprecated. Defines text font, size, and color*
<form>	3.0	3.0	STF	*Defines a form*
<frame>	3.0	3.0	F	*Defines a sub window (a frame)*
<frameset>	3.0	3.0	F	*Defines a set of frames*
<h1> to <h6>	3.0	3.0	STF	*Defines header 1 to header 6*
<head>	3.0	3.0	STF	*Defines information about the document*
<hr>	3.0	3.0	STF	*Defines a horizontal rule*
<html>	3.0	3.0	STF	*Defines an html document*
<i>	3.0	3.0	STF	*Defines italic text*
<iframe>	6.0	4.0	TF	*Defines an inline sub window (frame)*
<img>	3.0	3.0	STF	*Defines an image*
<input>	3.0	3.0	STF	*Defines an input field*
<ins>	6.2	4.0	STF	*Defines inserted text*
<isindex>	3.0	3.0	TF	*Deprecated. Defines a single-line input field*
<kbd>	3.0	3.0	STF	*Defines keyboard text*
<label>	6.2	4.0	STF	*Defines a label for a form control*
<legend>	6.2	4.0	STF	*Defines a title in a fieldset*
<li>	3.0	3.0	STF	*Defines a list item*
<link>	4.0	3.0	STF	*Defines a resource reference*
<map>	3.0	3.0	STF	*Defines an image map*
<menu>	3.0	3.0	TF	*Deprecated. Defines a menu list*
<meta>	3.0	3.0	STF	*Defines meta information*
<noframes>	3.0	3.0	TF	*Defines a noframe section*
<noscript>	3.0	3.0	STF	*Defines a noscript section*
<object>		3.0	STF	*Defines an embedded object*
<ol>	3.0	3.0	STF	*Defines an ordered list*
<optgroup>	6.0	6.0	STF	*Defines an option group*
<option>	3.0	3.0	STF	*Defines an option in a drop-down list*
<p>	3.0	3.0	STF	*Defines a paragraph*
<param>	3.0	3.0	STF	*Defines a parameter for an object*
<pre>	3.0	3.0	STF	*Defines preformatted text*

Tag				Description
<q>	6.2		STF	*Defines a short quotation*
<s>	3.0	3.0	TF	*Deprecated. Defines strikethrough text*
<samp>	3.0	3.0	STF	*Defines sample computer code*
<script>	3.0	3.0	STF	*Defines a script*
<select>	3.0	3.0	STF	*Defines a selectable list*
<small>	3.0	3.0	STF	*Defines small text*
<span>	4.0	3.0	STF	*Defines a section in a document*
<strike>	3.0	3.0	TF	*Deprecated. Defines strikethrough text*
<strong>	3.0	3.0	STF	*Defines strong text*
<style>	4.0	3.0	STF	*Defines a style definition*
<sub>	3.0	3.0	STF	*Defines subscripted text*
<sup>	3.0	3.0	STF	*Defines superscripted text*
<table>	3.0	3.0	STF	*Defines a table*
<tbody>		4.0	STF	*Defines a table body*
<td>	3.0	3.0	STF	*Defines a table cell*
<textarea>	3.0	3.0	STF	*Defines a text area*
<tfoot>		4.0	STF	*Defines a table footer*
<th>	3.0	3.0	STF	*Defines a table header*
<thead>		4.0	STF	*Defines a table header*
<title>	3.0	3.0	STF	*Defines the document title*
<tr>	3.0	3.0	STF	*Defines a table row*
<tt>	3.0	3.0	STF	*Defines teletype text*
<u>	3.0	3.0	TF	*Deprecated. Defines underlined text*
<ul>	3.0	3.0	STF	*Defines an unordered list*
<var>	3.0	3.0	STF	*Defines a variable*
<xmp>	3.0	3.0		*Deprecated. Defines preformatted text*

Other Works by the Author

You can find all these titles at *www.PracticalBooks.org.*

How to Destroy Your Debts
ISBN: 1-4116-2374-6

The Practical Guide to Total Financial Freedom: Volume 1
ISBN: 1-4116-2058-5

The Practical Guide to Total Financial Freedom: Volume 2
ISBN: 1-4116-2057-7

The Practical Guide to Total Financial Freedom: Volume 3
ISBN: 1-4116-2056-9

The Practical Guide to Total Financial Freedom: Volume 4
ISBN: 1-4116-2055-0

The Practical Guide to Total Financial Freedom: Volume 5
ISBN: 1-4116-2054-2

Planning and Goal Setting For Personal Success
ISBN: 1-4116-3774-7

Living the Ultimate Truth, 2nd Edition
ISBN: 1-4116-2375-4

Developing Personal Integrity, 2nd Edition
ISBN: 1-4116-2376-2

The Guide to Real Estate Investing
ISBN: 1-4116-2383-5

Tax Avoidance: A practical guide for UK Residents
ISBN: 1-4116-2380-0

Making Money with Funds
ISBN: 1-4116-2671-0

How to make a fortune with Options trading
ISBN: 1-4116-2378-9

How to make a fortune on the Stock Markets
ISBN: 1-4116-2379-7

Attitude
ISBN: 1-4116-2382-7

How to Win at Online Roulette
ISBN: 1-4116-2570-6

The Ultimate Guide to Offshore Tax Havens
ISBN: 1-4116-2384-3

How to win at Greyhound betting
ISBN: 1-4116-2377-0

Sixty Original Song Lyrics
ISBN: 1-4116-2059-3

Images of Kilimanjaro
CALENDAR: 12 months

Investing in En Primeur Wine
ISBN: 1-4116-2867-5

Eight Steps to Success
ISBN: 1-4116-2738-5

Taking Action
ISBN: 1-4116-2735-0

The Heart of Moscow (Calendar)
CALENDAR: 12 months

Paris 2006 (Calendar)
CALENDAR: 12 months

Ultimate Online Roulette System: Advanced Winning Techniques for the Tax Conscious Casino Gambling Investor
ISBN: 1-4116-4374-7

Naughty Madge Goes To A Farm
ISBN: 978-1-905789-97-9

The Kolumbas Affair
ISBN: 978-1-905789-99-3

ABOUT THE AUTHOR

Samuel Blankson has authored over twenty books, *The Kolumbas Affair, How to Destroy Your Debts, Living the Ultimate Truth, Developing Personal Integrity, The Practical Guide to Total Financial Freedom* volumes 1, 2, 3, 4 and 5, and *Attitude* are some of these works. He has also authored Children's books, fiction novels and a range of calendars. He has written over 100 songs, sixty of which are featured in *Sixty Original Song Lyrics*. Samuel Blankson's books can be found at ***www.practicalbooks.org***.